DISCOVERING HUMPBACK WHALES OF HAWAII

125 FUN FACTS ABOUT
HUMPBACKS

Paul Forestell and Gregory D. Kaufman

ISLAND HERITAGE™
PUBLISHING

Dedicated to our "keiki":
Cathy, Jordan, Makena and Ian
U'ilani, La'akea, Pūlama and Kūlia

"Answers are just bus stops you wait at,
until the next question comes along."
—*Fern Tingle*

Acknowledgments:

This book was inspired by Aurelio (Italian) and Maja (Swiss), founders of the beautiful Hosteria (Hotel) Mandela in Puerto Lopez, Ecuador. Puerto Lopez is the coastal home Machalilla National Marine Park, where southern hemisphere humpback whales gather to mate from June to September. As an ardent admirer of whales and Pacific Whale Foundation's work in Ecuador, Aurelio resolved to build the "Via Ballena"—a palm tree-lined road near his hosteria framed with educational humpback facts. The facts are complete with signs written in four languages—Spanish, Italian, French, and English– detailing a variety of facts about humpback whales.

Inspired after compiling the facts for Aurelio's signs, Pacific Whale Foundation expanded them into a full-length book for Hawai'i's locals and visitors. May the Via Ballena and this book stand as testaments to the enduring value of whales and the ocean in which they live.

Alicia Mallo, Chad Kruzic, and Anne Rillero provided research, design, and editorial support to make this book more accurate, attractive, and well written.

ISLAND HERITAGE™
P U B L I S H I N G
A DIVISION OF THE MADDEN CORPORATION

94-411 Kō'aki Street, Waipahu, Hawai'i 96797
Orders: (800) 468-2800 • Information: (808) 564-8800
Fax: (808) 564-8877
islandheritage.com

ISBN: 1-59700-309-3
First Edition, Third Printing, 2010

TABLE OF CONTENTS

INTRODUCTION

Cetaceans (whales, dolphins, and porpoises) are fascinating creatures, having evolved from land mammals over 60 million years, while developing remarkable adaptations to enable them to live throughout the world's oceans.

Many species of cetaceans live in Hawai'i, but perhaps the most visible and spectacular is the friendly humpback whale that visits here each winter. The Hawaiian Islands comprise the most significant breeding grounds for humpback whales in the entire North Pacific, and portions of the island chain are important enough to have become part of the Hawaiian Islands Humpback Whale National Marine Sanctuary—the only federal sanctuary in U.S. waters devoted to protecting humpback whales.

As leaders in whale research, marine education, and conservation, and as participants in the creation of Hawai'i's whale sanctuary, the Pacific Whale Foundation has devoted more than 25 years to fostering greater human understanding and appreciation of Hawai'i's humpback whales.

We offer this guide featuring interesting facts and stunning photos to help you learn about the anatomy, physiology, migratory patterns, and behaviors of humpbacks. We hope you will enjoy this information. Once you have read it, we invite you on the adventure of a lifetime—a fully narrated whale watch aboard one of the Pacific Whale Foundation's fleet of modern, whale-friendly vessels. We guarantee you an exciting journey as you experience for yourself the amazing world of whales.

Even if you can't come to Hawai'i for an up-close experience with this magnificent animal, we encourage you to contact the Pacific Whale Foundation for further information about cetaceans and the marine life of the Pacific. The ocean has been home to whales and dolphins for 60 million years; we invite you to join the foundation's efforts to ensure the marine environment will survive the threats presented by humans during the past two centuries.

We hope you enjoy this treasure chest of facts about one of the ocean's most energetic and friendly creatures—the magnificent humpback whale. Thank you for your interest in our work.

Paul H. Forestell
Gregory D. Kaufman

MIGRATION and DISTRIBUTION

1. Humpback whales, found in all oceans of the world, migrate annually from summer feeding grounds in polar oceans to winter breeding grounds near the tropics. While in the breeding grounds, they are usually found in water less than 600 feet deep.

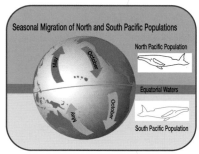

Seasonal Migration of North and South Pacific Populations

North Pacific Population

Equatorial Waters

South Pacific Population

May   October   October   May

2. North Pacific humpback whales use the waters around the Hawaiian Islands for breeding and calving from November to May. They spend the summer months feeding in Alaska's coastal waters.

3. Nearly 75 percent of the humpbacks that come to Hawai'i in the winter can be found in Maui County waters.

4

It is not clear why humpback whales migrate to Hawai'i during the breeding and calving season. One hypothesis is that it might protect newborn calves from predation by orca (killer) whales and large oceanic sharks, which are not found in large numbers near tropical shore waters.

5

The humpbacks that migrate to Hawai'i do not all arrive and depart at the same time. The first whales to appear are females with their yearlings (last year's calves), followed by juveniles of both sexes, then sexually active adult males and females. Females in late pregnancy are among the last whales to arrive.

6 At the end of the winter migration, humpbacks begin moving back to the feeding grounds. Newly pregnant females leave first, followed by juveniles, then adult males and females. Mothers with newborn calves are among the last to leave, when the calves have developed sufficiently to undertake their first long journey.

7
Young whales of both sexes follow experienced females to learn how to migrate between the feeding and breeding areas. Immature whales frequently travel together in small groups of two or three animals.

8 Male humpbacks range throughout the North Pacific, while females return to the same feeding and breeding areas each year.

9 Individual whales are transient in their movements among the main Hawaiian Islands. They spend only a few days at a time in any given location.

10 Humpback whales in the North Pacific do not generally cross the equator to intermingle with South Pacific populations. The breeding and feeding seasons are six months out of phase between the hemispheres.

11 Humpback whales travel three to five miles per hour during migration. They take from 30 to 60 days to travel between the feeding and breeding areas.

12 Humpback whales are distant cousins of the hippopotamus, having diverged from a common ancestor nearly 60 million years ago.

13 The scientific name for the humpback whale is *Megaptera novaeangliae* ("big-winged New Englander"). The name was based on its long pectoral fins when the species was first described in the Northeast Atlantic. The common name *humpback* refers to its habit of arching its back high above the water before it dives.

14 Humpback whales generally grow to 40 to 50 feet in length. Females are on average 3 to 5 feet longer than males.

15 Humpback whales have the longest pectoral fins of any whale or dolphin. They can be as long as 15 feet or up to one-third of their body length.

16 Adult humpback whales weigh 40 to 45 tons, with females on average larger than males.

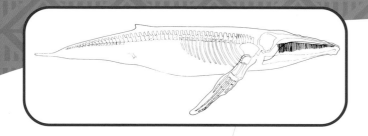

17 A humpback's bones comprise only 15 percent of its total body weight, compared with 50 percent in humans.

18 There are two types of whales, those with teeth and those with baleen (long, rigid strips of fingernail-like material suspended from the whale's upper jaw). Sperm and orca whales are both toothed (Odontocete) species. Humpback, blue, and right whales are examples of baleen (Mysticete) species.

19 Whales do not breathe through their mouth, but through a "blowhole" in the top of the head. Humpbacks, like all baleen whales, breathe through a blowhole that has two openings (similar to nostrils). Toothed whales and dolphins have only one opening in the blowhole.

20 Humpback whales have a series of 15 to 25 longitudinal grooves called ventral pleats along the throat, which allow them to stretch their mouth while feeding.

21
An adult humpback tongue weighs more than a ton. Although it is used to swallow food, it has little in the way of muscle structure and can't be extended beyond the mouth.

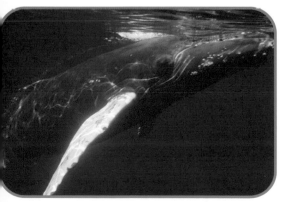

22
Humpbacks have a 14-inch wax earplug to prevent water from being forced into the ear canal and middle ear.

23
Humpback whales have tail flukes, which they use to propel themselves through the water with an up-and-down motion. The flukes can measure up to 15 feet wide.

24 To increase swimming efficiency, whales have no external earflaps or hind limbs. In addition, the genitalia and mammary glands, which are seven feet long and two feet wide in humpbacks, are completely encased within the body cavity.

25

When a humpback whale breathes, air rushes out of the blowhole at nearly 300 miles per hour.

26 Humpback whales are voluntary breathers, meaning they do not have a breathing reflex. If knocked unconscious, they will suffocate and die.

27 A swimming humpback breathes more frequently (every 6 to 8 minutes) than a resting whale (every 10 to 20 minutes). Singing males, however, can hold their breath for as long as an hour.

28 Humpbacks can hold their breath so long because their blood is rich in hemoglobin, a mechanism for storing oxygen in the blood.

29
Humpback whales are known as *rorquals* (Norwegian for "red whales") because their deep red blood gives a pinkish glow to the white areas of their throat and belly.

30 When a humpback whale defecates it creates a huge cloud of yellowish brown material that quickly dissipates in the water. We do not often see this in Hawai'i as they are not feeding while here.

31 Like all mammals, humpback whales need freshwater to survive, which they obtain from the fish they eat and from their stored fat reserves. While they do not actively drink seawater, they undoubtedly swallow some while feeding.

32 A humpback's blubber, which makes up approximately 30 percent of its body weight, stores energy and conserves body heat. It can be up to seven inches thick.

33 Humpbacks don't sweat. They control internal body temperature by regulating the extent to which cool blood returning to the heart is warmed by blood pumping away from the heart.

34 Humpback whales can live for more than 50 years, although 35 to 40 years is the average life expectancy.

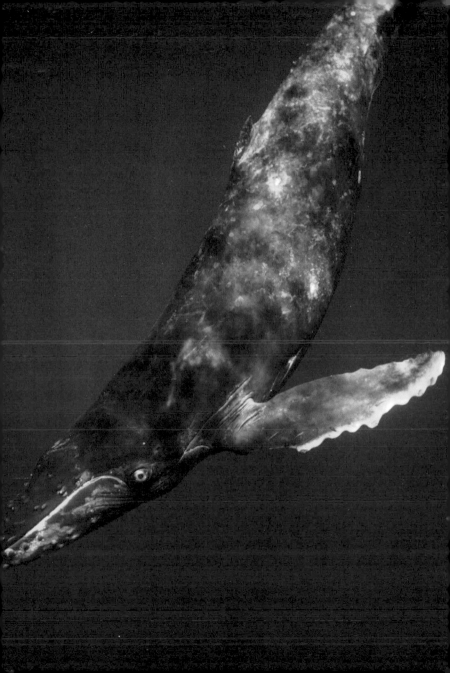

35 A humpback brain weighs 14 pounds, nearly five times the weight of a human brain. A sperm whale's 20-pound brain is the largest of any known animal.

36 Humpbacks rest with one hemisphere of the brain relaxed, while the other half continues to control body processes and maintain limited vigilance.

37 Humpback whale eyes have a specially shaped cornea and lens that permit excellent vision both above the water and below its surface.

38 A humpback's hearing is even more important than its vision for communication. Sound travels much farther underwater than light.

39

Human noise in the sea from large ships, oil exploration, and military exercises disturbs the humpback's ability to communicate and navigate. In some cases, loud noise causes serious damage to the structure of the inner ear.

40

Humpback whales do not have functional vocal cords. However, their larynx is well developed and contains a large chamber called the diverticulum. Whales force air past the chamber and folds of the larynx and into the rigid nasal passages, creating pressure fluctuations that generate sound.

41

Humpback whales have many knobby bumps known as tubercles (or "stove bolts" in whaling times) around their head. Each one has a single hair growing out of it, which may help detect motion or sound vibrations.

42 Although toothed whales and dolphins use echolocation (high-frequency sounds bounced off objects to return an echo) to navigate and locate objects underwater, baleen whales like the humpback do not.

43 Humpback whales have a poor sense of smell because their brain lacks olfactory bulbs, the necessary organs for smell.

44

Humpback whales show distinct preferences for eating certain species of fish, leading scientists to believe they have a well-developed sense of taste.

45 Humpback whales have no functional teeth. They have 300 to 400 strips of baleen hanging from the upper jaw, which they use to filter their prey from the ocean.

46 Adult humpbacks eat tiny shrimp-like crustaceans called krill, and small schooling fish like herring, capelin, sand lance, and mackerel.

47
Humpbacks can disconnect the lower jaw while feeding, opening their mouth more than 90 degrees. By stretching the ventral pleats, they can also enlarge the mouth to four times its normal size.

48 Humpback whales have a variety of feeding styles. They release bubbles from their blowhole in clouds, nets, or lines to disorient and concentrate prey.

49 Humpback whales often feed in groups of up to 15 animals. A lead animal uses a unique feeding sound and bubble nets to coordinate activities of the group.

50 Adult humpback whales consume more than a ton of food per day while feeding in Alaska. Cold polar waters support an explosion of prey species during the summer months.

51 Humpback whales do not eat in Hawai'i, where there is limited access to large schools of prey. They live off their blubber reserves and may lose 20 percent of their body weight during this forced winter fasting.

52 After feeding all summer, an adult humpback's blubber may be five to seven inches thick. By the end of the breeding season, it may be less than two inches thick.

53 Hawaiian humpbacks may feed during migration if sufficient prey is available. Pacific Whale Foundation scientists have observed feeding off Australia and Ecuador during the South Pacific humpback migration to the Antarctic feeding grounds.

PARASITES AND PREDATORS

54

Humpbacks have ectoparasites, which attach to the surface of the skin (such as barnacles), and endoparasites, which burrow beneath the epidermal layer and infest many internal organs and cavities (flatworms such as tapeworms, and roundworms such as hookworms). Humpback whales even have their own parasite (Haematophagus megapterae), found on no other animal. It digs into the baleen and feeds on blood cells.

55 Barnacles and sucker fish (such as remora) attach to humpback whales but do not directly feed off them. They feed on microorganisms in the ocean as the whale moves about.

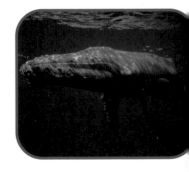

56

Humpback whales may have up to a ton of barnacles attached to their head and flippers when they leave the feeding grounds. Many of these fall off in warmer water.

57

Humpbacks in Hawai'i can be observed with small dolphins and toothed whales bow-riding at their head as they surface to breathe. However, the humpbacks appear to be disturbed by this.

58

Sharks and orca (killer) whales are the primary natural predators of humpback whales. Pacific Whale Foundation scientists have documented orca attacks on calves near both the breeding and feeding areas.

59

There has been an increase in sightings of orca whales near the Hawaiian Islands in recent years. Perhaps they are drawn here by the increasing numbers of migrating humpback whales recovering from the effects of commercial whaling.

60

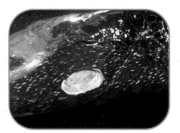

Many humpbacks bear the circular scars from puncture wounds caused by a small shark called the "cookie-cutter" shark.

61

A humpback whale's primary means of protection from predators is its powerful tail, which an angry whale may pound on the ocean's surface, or slash about like a giant karate chop.

62

Commercial whalers have killed more humpback whales than any natural predator. The pre-whaling population of North Pacific humpback whales (estimated at more than 20,000) was reduced to fewer than 1,000 by the mid-1970s. Commercial hunting of humpback whales is now illegal.

63

A female humpback's pregnancy lasts from 11 to 13 months.

64

No one has ever documented the birth of a humpback whale. On at least two occasions humpback placentas have been found off Maui, and scientists regularly observe small light gray calves. There is little doubt the calves are born on or near the breeding grounds.

65

Female whales usually give birth to one calf at a time because pregnancy, birth, and nursing demand tremendous resources.

66

Female humpbacks generally give birth every two years and rest for a year between births. However, a small number of females have been observed with newborn calves in consecutive years.

67 The overall sex ratio of newborn male to female calves is estimated at roughly 50:50.

68
A newborn humpback calf is 12 to 15 feet long and weighs approximately one and a half tons.

69 A humpback whale grows to about 30 feet within the first year.

70
A newborn calf rises naturally to the surface for air, but must learn with its mother's help how to dive below the surface and control its buoyancy.

71

Calves usually surface to breathe every three to four minutes, while their mothers stay down for at least twice as long.

72 A calf does not suckle milk from its mother because the tongue lacks the necessary muscle structure. Pressure from the calf's mouth pushing against the nipple, when exposed through the mammary slit, causes the mother to squirt milk directly into her baby's mouth.

73 A humpback mother's milk is very high in fat content, containing as much as 40 percent fat, compared with 4 percent in humans.

74 A newborn calf can drink as much as 100 gallons of milk a day.

75 Mothers with newborn calves avoid each other soon after giving birth so they do not inadvertently feed their valuable milk to the wrong calf.

76

Females begin weaning their calves toward the end of their first summer feeding period in Alaska, in preparation for the return migration to the wintering grounds.

77

Humpback calves have a relatively small mouth (15 percent of body length) compared with adults (25 to 30 percent). A strong tail is more important than a big mouth for newborns, since they have to swim well immediately, but will not begin capturing fish for nearly a year and a half.

78

Copulation in humpbacks, as with all mammals, involves internal fertilization. However, intromission has never actually been observed in Hawai'i. Paternity can only be determined through genetic analysis.

79

Male and female humpback genital areas look similar, except the female has a large bump called a hemispherical lobe at the tail end of the genital slit. The distance between the anus and the genital slit is greater on males than on females.

80

Although normally retracted within the body cavity, the penis of a humpback male is approximately eight feet in length when fully extended.

81

Humpback whales reach sexual maturity (similar to puberty in humans) by the time they are 7 or 8 years of age, but appear not to become sexually active (mating and giving birth) until 5 or more years later.

82

Humpback whales do not mate for life. Females mate with a number of different males during each breeding season.

83

There are more reproductively active males attempting to breed than ovulating females available to breed at any given time during the winter, leading to intense competition among males. Only the most dominant male humpbacks (based on size and fitness) will successfully mate.

84 Although female humpbacks can ovulate multiple times during the breeding season, only a portion of reproductively active females will be in heat at one time.

85 Female humpbacks normally get pregnant in Hawai'i and give birth here upon their return the following year. Though they typically rest a year between births, females can get pregnant immediately after giving birth.

86

The peak of the breeding season is from February through March. This is when we in Hawai'i hear the greatest number of singers, count the highest number of whales, and observe the largest and most competitive groups, or pods, of whales.

87 Humpbacks are the most acrobatic of the great whales. In Hawai'i, the behaviors we see are primarily associated with male competition, mating, and calf rearing.

88
When competing for females, a male "primary escort" stays close to the female and keeps other males away. "Challengers" try to displace the primary escort.

89 Eighty percent of mother and calf pods in Hawai'i are accompanied by an escort, which is not the father of the calf. Its association with the mother and calf lasts only a few hours, perhaps because lactating females do not usually ovulate and are therefore not potential mates.

90

Male humpback whales use many displays (tail slaps, head slaps, and explosive underwater blows) to threaten each other in battles for access to females.

91

The most aggressive display scientists have witnessed is the peduncle slap. The whale throws the entire rear half of its body above the surface and slams it down sideways in an explosive display. This behavior is usually directed toward another whale or a boat.

92

Although referred to as "gentle giants," humpbacks use their head and tail as formidable weapons. Older male whales show many scars and bloody cuts from their competitive encounters. On one occasion observed, an adult male died during a competitive bout.

93 Pectoral fin displays may be signals of invitation. By waving and slapping their fins on the surface, mothers appear to keep their calves from wandering away, and courting males and females encourage each other's efforts.

94

Humpback whales are capable of spectacular leaps above the surface, a behavior called breaching. This high-energy display signals an animal's location, fitness, and emotional state. Scientists also believe it allows visual scanning above the surface, and that often whales might breach simply because it's fun.

95 Whale watchers are frequently delighted when a whale slowly emerges head first, exposing its eye above the water, a behavior known as spy hopping.

SONG

96
Both males and females make a variety of social sounds, but only male humpbacks sing. The song is primarily heard during winter on the breeding grounds.

97
The social sounds of humpback whales include snores, coughs, squeaks, rumbles, and trumpet blows, which can be heard both above and below the surface.

98
While singing, a male humpback holds its breath and stays submerged for as long as it can. Downtimes range from eight minutes to an hour, and may correlate with the animal's fitness.

99
A singing whale usually remains suspended at 50 to 70 feet with its head down and tail up. It stays relatively motionless except for a gentle sculling of the pectoral fins. Occasionally humpbacks sing while swimming along with other whales or during migration.

100
Underwater listening devices, or hydrophones, can detect the song of the male humpback whale from many miles away. Scientists have determined that more males sing at night than during the day.

101

Humpback song is a complex, orderly sequence of many sounds comprising a series of phrases. Up to 20 minutes long, the song can be repeated over and over for many hours.

102

Different populations of humpback whales around the world sing different songs, but all the males within a population sing the same song.

103

The song undergoes slight but detectable changes by the end of each breeding season. When whales return the following year, they begin singing the version that was in vogue at the end of the previous season.

104

The specific sequence and structure of a given population's song evolve over a series of years, so that eventually a completely new song emerges.

105

The function of the humpback song is not known with certainty. It may signal fitness or readiness to mate, establish territory, or serve as a challenge to other males.

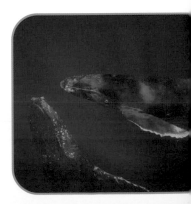

106 The first extended underwater observations of humpback whales took place off Maui in 1974 by Jim Hudnall, a freelance photographer and amateur whale researcher.

107

Each humpback whale has a unique pattern of marks and pigmentation on the undersurface of the tail flukes, which Pacific Whale Foundation scientists photograph to identify individual animals. Long-term case histories of known whales can then be documented.

108

Resights of individual humpbacks photographically identified in Hawai'i have been documented in Japan, Alaska, California, and Mexico. In 1986, scientists photographed a male humpback off Kaua'i that was photographed seven weeks earlier off the coast of Mexico. This is the only known instance of a humpback whale moving between breeding grounds within the same season.

109

Local movement patterns can be tracked by shore-based observers using computerized surveyor's equipment. Long-term movements, however, require use of satellite transmitters and remote underwater listening stations.

110

When whales engage in high-energy activities like breaches and tail slaps, they leave small pieces of skin in the water. Genetic analysis of this material helps determine gender, paternity, level of accumulated biotoxins, and degree of relatedness between populations.

111 Humpback whales in Hawai'i are more darkly pigmented on the underneath surface of their body than the whales found in the South Pacific.

112

The fictional Moby Dick was an albino (all-white) sperm whale. The only documented albino humpback whale was spotted in 1991 off the eastern coast of Australia, and has been observed many times since. It was given the name Migaloo (Aboriginal for "white fellow") by Pacific Whale Foundation.

CONSERVATION and RECOVERY

113 Prior to commercial whaling, there were hundreds of thousands of humpback whales throughout the world. Today there may be fewer than 50,000, although their numbers continue to increase since the cessation of commercial whaling.

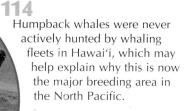

114 Humpback whales were never actively hunted by whaling fleets in Hawai'i, which may help explain why this is now the major breeding area in the North Pacific.

115 Approximately 6,000 to 8,000 humpback whales come to Hawai'i each year. This represents approximately 60 percent of the North Pacific population.

116 Aerial surveys have documented annual increases in Hawai'i humpback whale numbers that suggest the population will double within the next 15 years.

117

Part of the Hawaiian breeding ground is included within the Hawaiian Islands Humpback Whale National Marine Sanctuary, where federal and state agencies work with non-profit organizations like Pacific Whale Foundation to educate the public about the recovery status of the humpback whale.

118

Throughout Hawaiian waters, federal law prohibits harassing whales or approaching them closer than 100 yards. Boaters are advised to reduce their speeds when a whale is sighted, and to avoid staying near a mother and calf for more than 30 minutes.

119

Humpback whales are protected from commercial whaling, but many die each year from accidental ship strikes and net entanglement. Other threats through-out their migratory range include human activities that generate biotoxins, noise, marine debris, over-fishing, and habitat loss or degradation.

120

As the population of whales increases in Hawai'i, it may be necessary to introduce speed limits and trained observers on large ships and ferries to reduce the risk of ship strikes.

121

One of the greatest sources of disturbance to humpback whales is acoustic harassment. The use of low-frequency sonar as part of military operations is of growing concern to Pacific Whale Foundation and other environmental groups.

122

Pacific Whale Foundation uses the latest technology to build whale watch vessels that reduce noise, increase fuel efficiency, and provide better viewing platforms for passengers.

123

A humpback whale can live for 50 years, with the chance of being seen many times by whale watchers. It can be killed only once, which is why whale watching is more economically valuable than whaling.

124

Whale watching currently generates $20 million a year in Hawai'i and more than $1 billion worldwide. Each year nearly 350,000 people watch whales in Hawai'i.

125

Pacific Whale Foundation's research, education, and conservation programs are based on the conviction that a well-informed public is the best defense against the extinction of Hawai'i's humpback whales.

ABOUT THE PACIFIC WHALE FOUNDATION

In 1980, Hawai'i's humpback whales were facing extinction. A young man named Greg Kaufman founded the nonprofit Pacific Whale Foundation, an organization devoted to saving whales and protecting their ocean home through research, conservation, and education.

Today, Pacific Whale Foundation is Hawai'i's oldest and largest marine conservation organization, with over a quarter century of proud accomplishments. Thousands of humpback whales have been individually photo-identified by the foundation's research team. Working in Ecuador, Australia, Hawai'i, Japan, and other parts of the Pacific, they provide valuable data on whale populations, migration, and social dynamics.

The foundation has helped to establish protected areas for whales in Australia, Hawai'i, and Ecuador. It has fought to protect whales throughout the Pacific through legislation and education. And it continues to identify serious problems that threaten whales and their habitat. These include LFA sonar, marine debris, CO_2 dumping in Hawai'i, vessel collisions with whales, overfishing, and habitat loss. Recognizing we can't protect whales if we don't protect their home, the foundation's research, conservation, and education efforts have expanded to include coral reefs, turtles, and toothed whales and dolphins.

Over two million people have learned about whales and the oceans through Pacific Whale Foundation's innovative ecotours, which promote ecofriendly interactions with the marine environment and teach stewardship of the ocean. Its Ocean Science Discovery Center on Maui serves thousands of schoolchildren each year through award-winning programs.

For more information about Pacific Whale Foundation, visit www.pacificwhale.org; e-mail info@pacificwhale.org; or write Pacific Whale Foundation, 300 Māʻalaea Road, Suite 211, Wailuku, Hawaiʻi 96793.

ABOUT THE AUTHORS

Paul H. Forestell, Ph.D., is professor of psychology and animal behavior at Long Island University in New York. He is also vice president and senior research associate of the Pacific Whale Foundation. Born in Canada and educated at the University of New Brunswick, he received his Ph.D. from the University of Hawai'i in 1988. For 30 years, Paul has studied the cognitive and social behaviors of whales and dolphins throughout the Pacific. He joined the Pacific Whale Foundation in 1981, and gained international recognition for his understanding of the impacts of a rapidly expanding whale and dolphin watching industry, and his development of formal training programs for naturalists and educators associated with marine tourism. In addition to aerial and boat-based observations of humpback whales in Hawai'i and Australia, Paul has conducted whale watch workshops in Hawai'i, Australia, Japan, and Ecuador. He continues to study dolphins in Costa Rica, and humpback whales in Ecuador and Australia.

Gregory D. Kaufman is the founder and president of the Pacific Whale Foundation. His efforts to protect whales began in the 1970s. Greg traveled throughout the United States and Europe, educating the public about the plight of endangered whales and demanding an end to commercial whaling. In 1975, he came to Hawai'i, the primary mating and calving area for humpback whales in the North Pacific, and began some of the first field studies of the behavior of live whales. A pioneer in noninvasive whale research, Greg founded the Pacific Whale Foundation in 1980, and committed his new organization to educating the public, from a scientific perspective, about whales and their ocean habitat. Since then, Greg has proven a leader in addressing whale protection issues. He has pioneered responsible whale and dolphin watching programs throughout the Pacific, and is widely acknowledged as an innovator and leader in marine ecotourism. Greg's work on humpback whales has taken him to every corner of the Pacific, and has resulted in the most complete and extensive catalog of humpback whale tail fluke identification photographs in the Southern Hemisphere.